## NATURAL WONDERS
# GREAT
# BARRIER REEF

by Katie Chanez

po go

# Ideas for Parents and Teachers

Pogo Books let children practice reading informational text while introducing them to nonfiction features such as headings, labels, sidebars, maps, and diagrams, as well as a table of contents, glossary, and index.

Carefully leveled text with a strong photo match offers early fluent readers the support they need to succeed.

## Before Reading

- "Walk" through the book and point out the various nonfiction features. Ask the student what purpose each feature serves.
- Look at the glossary together. Read and discuss the words.

## Read the Book

- Have the child read the book independently.
- Invite them to list questions that arise from reading.

## After Reading

- Discuss the child's questions. Talk about how they might find answers to those questions.
- Prompt the child to think more. Ask: Did you know about the Great Barrier Reef before reading this book? What more would you like to learn about it?

Pogo Books are published by Jump!
5357 Penn Avenue South
Minneapolis, MN 55419
www.jumplibrary.com

Library of Congress Cataloging-in-Publication Data

Names: Chanez, Katie, author.
Title: Great Barrier Reef / by Katie Chanez.
Description: Minneapolis, MN: Jump!, Inc., [2025]
Series: Natural wonders | Includes index.
Audience: Ages 7-10
Identifiers: LCCN 2024031638 (print)
LCCN 2024031639 (ebook)
ISBN 9798892135405 (hardcover)
ISBN 9798892135412 (paperback)
ISBN 9798892135429 (ebook)
Subjects: LCSH: Coral reef ecology—Australia—Great Barrier Reef (Qld.) —Juvenile literature. | Marine parks and reserves—Australia—Great Barrier Reef (Qld.) —Juvenile literature. | Coral reef animals—Australia—Great Barrier Reef (Qld.) —Juvenile literature. | Marine animals—Australia—Great Barrier Reef (Qld.) —Juvenile literature. | Great Barrier Reef (Qld.) —Juvenile literature. Great Barrier Reef (Qld.) —History—Juvenile literature.
Classification: LCC QE566.G7 C43 2025 (print)
LCC QE566.G7 (ebook)
DDC 577.7/8909943—dc23/eng20240814
LC record available at https://lccn.loc.gov/2024031638
LC ebook record available at https://lccn.loc.gov/2024031639

Editor: Alyssa Sorenson
Designer: Molly Ballanger

Photo Credits: marcobrivio.photography/Shutterstock, cover, 5; AtifulRehman/Shutterstock, 1; Jolanta Wojcicka/Shutterstock, 3; Islandjems - Jemma Craig/Shutterstock, 4; Tunatura/Shutterstock, 6-7; dream02/Shutterstock, 8; Milano M/Shutterstock, 9; Naeemphotographer2/Shutterstock, 10-11; aquapix/Shutterstock, 12-13; Sipa USA/Alamy, 14; DAVID GRAY/AFP/Getty, 15; Nigel Marsh/iStock, 16-17tl; ChameleonsEye/Shutterstock, 16-17tr; William Edge/Shutterstock, 16-17 (bottom); Rob Atherton/Dreamstime, 18-19tl; Nicram Sabod/Shutterstock, 18-19tr; Michael Smith ITWP/Shutterstock, 18-19bl; Theresa J Graham/Shutterstock, 18-19br; mroz/iStock, 20-21; EQRoy/Shutterstock, 23.

Printed in the United States of America at Corporate Graphics in North Mankato, Minnesota.

# TABLE OF CONTENTS

# CHAPTER 1

# LIFE ON THE REEF

Bright fish swim off the coast of Australia. **Coral** offers hiding spots. Many animals call this place home. What is it? It is the Great **Barrier Reef**!

coral

The Great Barrier Reef is 1,429 miles (2,300 kilometers) long. It is in the Coral Sea.

The water is **shallow** and warm. Sunlight heats it. **Algae** live in the coral. They make and share food with the coral. Many types of coral make up the reef.

**DID YOU KNOW?**

The Great Barrier Reef is the only living thing visible from space!

# CHAPTER 2

······································································

# HOW IT FORMED

The Great Barrier Reef was not always here. About 20,000 years ago, this area was covered in forests.

This was during an **ice age**. Parts of Earth were covered in ice.

ice

AUSTRALIA

Earth 20,000 years ago

What changed? About 10,000 years ago, Earth got warmer. The ice melted. The **sea level** rose. Shallow water covered the area.

## DID YOU KNOW?

**Aboriginal** peoples once lived where the reef is now. Their **legends** tell of the land flooding.

The ocean carried coral **polyps** to the area. Polyps stuck to rocks and the seafloor. Each made a hard **exoskeleton**. They joined to make coral. The coral **reproduced**. They formed the reef. This happened between 8,000 and 6,000 years ago.

polyp

# TAKE A LOOK!

How does a coral reef form? Take a look!

**1** A coral polyp attaches to a rock or the seafloor.

**2** The polyp forms a hard exoskeleton.

**EXOSKELETON**

**3** It joins with other polyps to form a coral. The coral reproduces.

**4** The ocean carries more polyps to the area. A reef forms.

# CHAPTER 3

VISITING
THE REEF

Aboriginal peoples have lived near the reef for thousands of years. They share their **traditional** ways of life with others.

Europeans first explored the reef in 1770. It has been a popular place to visit ever since. More than 2 million people come each year! Some are scientists. They want to learn about the coral and other plants and animals that call this place home.

Some visitors come for fun! There are many things to do. Some scuba dive or snorkel. Others boat or swim.

**WHAT DO YOU THINK?**

Would you like to visit the Great Barrier Reef? Why or why not? What would you want to do here?

blue-ringed octopus

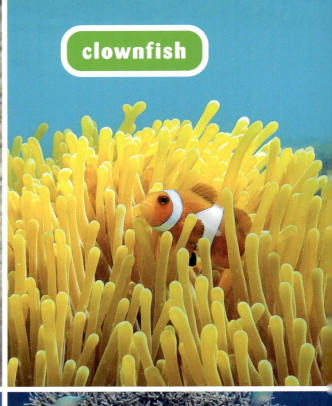

clownfish

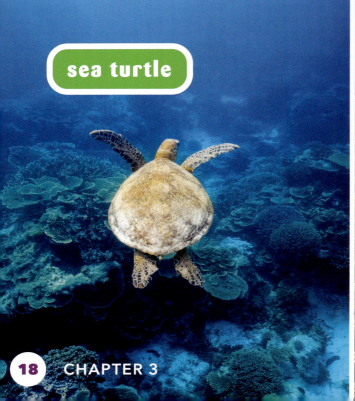

sea turtle

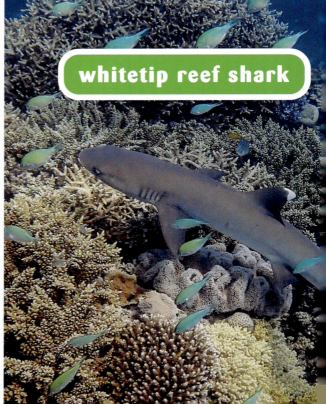

whitetip reef shark

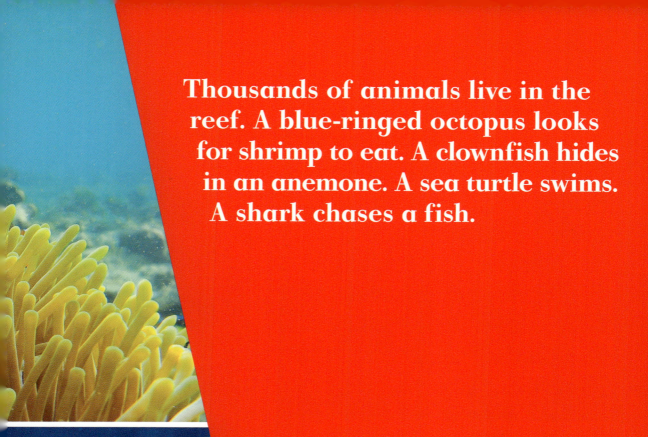

Thousands of animals live in the reef. A blue-ringed octopus looks for shrimp to eat. A clownfish hides in an anemone. A sea turtle swims. A shark chases a fish.

In 1975, the Australian government started protecting the reef. But it still faces threats. **Climate change** is making the ocean warmer. When this happens, the algae leave. The coral may die. Without coral, animals that live in the reef struggle. By protecting the reef, we can keep this a beautiful place!

## WHAT DO YOU THINK?

Coral reefs are not the only places threatened by climate change. What are some ways you can help fight climate change?

# QUICK FACTS & TOOLS

AT A GLANCE

## GREAT BARRIER REEF

**Location:**
off the coast of Australia

**Date Formed:**
about 8,000 to 6,000 years ago

**How It Formed:**
coral polyps grew and spread

**Number of Yearly Visitors:**
more than 2 million people

# GLOSSARY

**Aboriginal:** The native peoples of Australia who lived there before Europeans arrived.

**algae:** Small plants without roots or stems that grow mainly in water.

**barrier reef:** A group of coral that grows along a shore with a body of water between the shore and the coral.

**climate change:** Changes in weather and weather patterns that happen because of human activity.

**coral:** Small ocean animals that stay in one place and have hard exoskeletons.

**exoskeleton:** A hard covering on the outside of an animal.

**ice age:** A period of time in history when a large part of Earth was covered in ice.

**legends:** Stories that are handed down from earlier times.

**polyps:** Small sea animals with tubular bodies and round mouths surrounded by tentacles.

**reproduced:** Produced offspring.

**sea level:** The average height of Earth's oceans.

**shallow:** Not deep.

**traditional:** Having to do with customs, beliefs, or activities that are handed down from one generation to the next.

# INDEX

# TO LEARN MORE

Finding more information is as easy as 1, 2, 3.

1. Go to www.factsurfer.com
2. Enter "GreatBarrierReef" into the search box.
3. Choose your book to see a list of websites.

FACT SURFER